PRIVATE EYE

RUN FOR COVER

A COLLECTION OF THE BEST EYE COVERS FROM THE LAST FIVE YEARS

Published in Great Britain by Private Eye Productions Ltd
6 Carlisle Street, London W1V 5RG
in association with Corgi Books

© 1994 Pressdram Ltd
ISBN 0 552 14282 4
Designed by Bridget Tisdall
Printed in England by Ebenezer Baylis & Son Ltd, Worcester

Corgi Books are published by Transworld Publishers Ltd
61–63 Uxbridge Road, Ealing, London W5 5SA
in Australia by Transworld Publishers (Australia) Pty, Ltd
15–23 Helles Avenue, Moorebank, NSW 2170
and in New Zealand by Transworld Publishers (N.Z.) Ltd
3 William Pickering Drive, Albany, Auckland

2 4 6 8 10 9 7 5 3 1

After extravagant praise the Chancellor's policies begin to fall apart.

PRIVATE EYE

No. 716
Friday
26 May '89

50p

LAWSON'S ECONOMIC MIRACLE

Sonia Sutcliffe, the wife of the Yorkshire Ripper, is awarded a record £600,000 in libel damages against Private Eye.

PRIVATE EYE

No. 717
Friday
9 June '89

50p

The Foreign Secretary decides that only a very few of the six million subjects in Hong Kong will be allowed to move to Britain after 1997.

PRIVATE EYE

No. 719
Friday
7 July '89

60p

HOWE APPALLING

The English cricket team is repeatedly beaten
by the Australians.

PRIVATE EYE

722
day
Aug. '89

60p

ENGLAND'S SURPRISE TACTIC

Can you bowl underarm, please?

An Australian-American media tycoon makes a controversial speech.

PRIVATE SKY

o. 723
iday
Sept. '89

60p

MURDOCH LASHES OUT

Britain is class-ridden, elitist and snobbish, if I may say so, Your Royal Highness, Ma'am, grovel... grovel...

Princess Anne and Captain Mark Phillips
formally announce the end of their marriage.

PRIVATE EYE

No. 722
Friday
15 Sept. '89

60p

ROYAL SEPARATION
SOUVENIR SPECIAL 1973~1989

It's all been very amicable

There are increasing fears about the mental condition of the Prime Minister.

No. 728
Friday
0 Nov. '89

PRIVATE EYE

NOW 36 PAGES

60p

When Romanian dictator Nicolae Ceausescu is overthrown and executed, Britain is reminded that the Queen awarded him the KCMG.

No. 732
Friday
Jan. '90

60p

PRIVATE EYE

IT'S CIAO-SESCU !!

MEMORIAL ISSUE

Rival newspaper editors, Andrew Neil of the Sunday Times and Donald Trelford of the Observer, vie for the attentions of call girl Pamella Bordes.

No. 734
Friday
Feb. '90

60p

PRIVATE EYE

EDITOR IN LIBEL SHOCKER

Nelson Mandela is released after 27 years in prison.

PRIVATE EYE

No. 735
Friday
16 Feb. '90.

60p

Sentiments amongst the Cabinet begin to echo those of public demonstrations.

PRIVATE EYE

No. 737
Friday
16 March '90

60p

IT'S RENTAMOB

Inmates of Strangeways revolt.

PRIVATE EYE

No. 739
Friday
13 April '90.

60p

PRISON RIOTS LATEST

John Gummer counteracts BSE scare by feeding a burger to his daughter.

PRIVATE EYE

o. 742
riday
5 May '90

60p

"BEEF SAFE" — GUMMER

England manager Bobby Robson defends his team over allegations of sexual impropriety.

PRIVATE EYE

No. 744
Friday
22 June '90

60p

SEXY ISABELLA
Robson denies rumours

None of my lads has scored for years

INSIDE: FOUR PAGE FULL COLOUR SUNDAY TIMES COMIC!!

The Queen Mother celebrates her
90th birthday.

PRIVATE EYE

o. 747
riday
Aug. '90

70p

70-80-90 ! PHEW
WHAT A QUEEN MOTHER !

Saddam Hussein invades Kuwait.

PRIVATE EYE

o. 748
iday
Aug. '90

70p

The Chancellor of the Exchequer agrees with the Prime Minister, and takes Britain into the Exchange Rate Mechanism of the European Monetary System.

PRIVATE EYE

No. 752
Friday
12 Oct. '90

70p

MAJOR SAYS YES TO ERM

Former Prime Minister Edward Heath flies to Baghdad to negotiate for the release of British hostages.

PRIVATE EYE

No. 753
Friday
26 Oct. '90

70p

HEATH'S TRIUMPH

Mrs Thatcher is deposed.

PRIVATE EYE

No. 756   FRIDAY 7 DECEMBER 1990   70p

REJOICE ! REJOICE !

Thatcher Memorial Issue

40-PAGE BUMPER SPECIAL

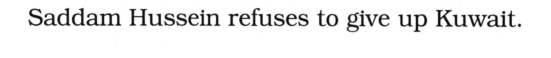

Saddam Hussein refuses to give up Kuwait.

PRIVATE EYE

o. 762
riday
March '91

70p

SADDAM'S LAST DITCH BID

A woman in New Zealand issues a paternity suit against Captain Mark Phillips after an alleged affair.

PRIVATE EYE

No. 764
Friday
March '91

70p

MARK ISSUES STATEMENT

American President George Bush is taken to hospital but assures reporters that he is fine.

PRIVATE EYE

No. 767
Friday
May '91
70p

BUSH HEART DRAMA

Mrs Thatcher keeps a dignified silence.

PRIVATE EYE

769
ay
ne '91

70p

As a famous jockey is convicted of defrauding the inland revenue, the Queen considers her own position.

PRIVATE EYE

o. 771
riday
July '91

70p

TAX:QUEEN SEEKS ADVICE

Gorbachev arrives at the G7 summit in London to ask for financial aid.

PRIVATE EYE

No. 772
Friday
19 July '91

70p

GORBY FLIES IN

Opera becomes popular.

PRIVATE EYE

No. 773
Friday
2 Aug. '91

70p

PAVAROTTI'S FREE CONCERT

The Archbishop of Canterbury attributes the recent riots to failings in economic and social policy.

o. 777
riday
Sept. '91

70p

PRIVATE EYE

CAREY RIOT SHOCK

Coronation Street actor Bill Roache starts a libel action over a newspaper's suggestion that he is boring.

PRIVATE EYE

No. 780
Friday
8 Nov. '91

80p

'STREET" STAR — LATEST

Robert Maxwell is buried.

PRIVATE BYE

80p

A NATION MOURNS

The Prime Minister enjoys a festive
photo-opportunity.

PRIVATE EYE

782
day
ec. '91

80p

Under the stewardship of Chancellor Norman Lamont sterling plummets.

No. 784
...day
...an. '92

PRIVATE EYE

80p

CHANCELLOR'S NEW
YEAR MESSAGE

The Prime Minster is honoured by Sue Lawley.

PRIVATE EYE

785
day
Jan. '92

80p

DESERT ISLAND DISCS

JOHN MAJOR'S CHOICE

The Duchess of York receives more unfavourable press coverage.

. 786
day
Jan. '92

PRIVATE EYE

80p

The Prime Minister is falsely accused of having an affair.

PRIVATE EYE

No. 787
Friday
14 Feb. '92

80p

MAJOR'S MISTRESS

●EXCLUSIVE PICTURE●

NEW SMEAR SHOCK

The Duke and Duchess of York decide to separate.

PRIVATE EYE

No. 790
Friday
27 March '92

80p

FERGIE'S HEARTACHE

£5 million or I go to the *Sun*

ROYAL DIVORCE SOUVENIR

Benny Hill and Frankie Howerd die.
Neil Kinnock and Roy Hattersley step down as
labour party leaders.

No. 792
Friday
April '92

PRIVATE EYE

80p

TWO TOP COMICS LOST
A NATION MOURNS

A possible solution to the Docklands crisis.

No. 794
Friday
22 May '92
80p

PRIVATE EYE

NEW HOME FOR FERGIE

CANARY WHARF SAVED

The nation welcomes a new Life Peer.

No. 796
Friday
June '92

PRIVATE EYE

80p

ARCHER HONOURED

As Virginia Bottomley warns against the dangers of teenage pregnancy it is revealed that she herself was a young single mother.

PRIVATE EYE

798
day
July '92

80p

BOTTOMLEY'S HEALTH WARNING

Watch out, girls — they're about this long and highly dangerous

David Mellor poses for a family photograph after his affair with actress Antonia de Sancha threatens his career.

PRIVATE EYE

o. 799
riday
July '92

80p

Western leaders continue to procrastinate over the civil war in the former Yugoslavia.

No. 800
Friday
14 Aug. '92

80p

PRIVATE EYE

The press publishes intimate photographs of
the Duchess of York and John Bryan.

PRIVATE EYE

o. 801
riday
8 Aug. '92
80p

FERGIE'S FINANCIAL ADVISER

Chancellor Norman Lamont loses the Treasury billions of pounds on Black Wednesday. Both he and David Mellor remain in the Cabinet.

PRIVATE EYE

No. 803
Friday
25 Sept. '92

80p

GOVERNMENT IN CRISIS

The Conservative conference does not go well
for the Prime Minister.

PRIVATE EYE

No. 805
Friday
3 Oct. '92

80p

MAJOR'S SUPPORT LOWEST EVER

Not only is the Chancellor revealed to have an outstanding Access bill, but it emerges that the Treasury paid his personal legal costs in evicting a tenant.

PRIVATE EYE

No. 808
Friday
Dec. '92

80p

LAMONT
NO CREDIT LEFT

The Prince and Princess of Wales decide to separate.

PRIVATE DI

YULETIDE GREETINGS

Tape recordings of a phone conversation between the Prince of Wales and Lady Camilla Parker-Bowles are made public.

PRIVATE EYE

CALLCUTT SPECIAL

812
May
an. '93

80p

CAMILLAGATE LATEST

The crisis in Bosnia continues.

PRIVATE EYE

o. 818
riday
April '93

80p

BOSNIA
MAJOR GETS TOUGH

When I give the order, do nothing at all

The Queen announces that Buckingham
Palace will be opened to the public in August.

PRIVATE EYE

No. 819
Friday
7 May '93

80p

YES! ITS THE PALACE OF FUN

Controversy rages over alleged listening devices placed in Buckingham Palace.

PRIVATE EYE

No. 820
Friday
21 May '93

80p

ROYAL BUGGING - NEW SHOCK

Kenneth Clarke replaces Norman Lamont as Chancellor of the Exchequer.

PRIVATE EYE

No. 821
Friday
June '93

80p

CLARKE IN – LAMONT OUT

Raine Spencer, daughter of Barbara Cartland and stepmother of Princess Diana, marries again.

PRIVATE EYE

o. 824
riday
5 July '93

90p

STILL
ONLY
90p

ROYAL WEDDING SOUVENIR

The corgis have the last word.

PRIVATE EYE

o. 826
riday
Aug. 93
90p

QUEEN FLEES AS BUCK HOUSE OPENS

The Government pushes ahead with its plans to privatise British Rail.

PRIVAT ISE

No. 827
Friday
27 Aug. '93

90p

BR SELL OFF Latest

Israel and the PLO sign a historic peace agreement.

No. 828
Friday
10 Sept. '93

PRIVATE EYE

90p

MIDDLE EAST LATEST

The Prime Minister's leadership crisis deepens.

PRIVATE EYE

No. 829
Friday
4 Sept. '93

90p

Still only 90p

DESPERATE MAJOR'S SHOCK PLEA

Support me or I'll hit you over the head with this hammer

Princess Diana takes action over press pictures of her in the gym taken by hidden camera.

PRIVATE EYE

No. 833
Friday
19 Nov. '93

90p

MORE CASH FOR SINGLE MOTHERS

I'm getting millions from the *Mirror*

Diana shock pix
Page 3

The President of the United States answers his critics.

PRIVATE EYE

No. 836
Friday
Dec. '93

90p

CLINTON DENIES SEX RUMOURS

Michael Heseltine emerges as the front runner in any potential leadership challenge but continues to pledge his support for the Prime Minister.

PRIVATE IDES

No. 841
Friday
1 March '92

90p

The Grand National coincides with intense speculation about a leadership challenge.

No. 843
Friday
April '94

90p

PRIVATE EYE

GRAND NATIONAL FIASCO

A man claims that he has been refused
treatment in hospital because he is too old.

PRIVATE EYE

No. 844
iday
April '94

90p

BOTTOMLEY IN OVER-65 SHOCKER

The Channel Tunnel is officially opened.

PRIVATE EYE

o. 845
riday
May '94

90p

HISTORY IS MADE
CHUNNEL OPEN!

We apologise for the late arrival of the 12.15 from Calais due to seaweed on the line

NEW £100 PRIZE CROSSWORD INSIDE

R. I. P.

PRIVATE EYE

No. 846
Friday
20 May '94

90p

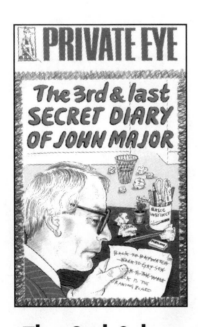